CELEBRATE WONDER

Includes One Room Sunday School®

Vol. 4 • No. 4 • Summer 2024

EDITORIAL / DESIGN TEAM

Selena Cunningham . . . . .Editor

Megan Teegarden. . . . . .Editor

Pamela Crosby . . . . Production Editor

Matt Allison . . . . . Production & Design Manager

ADMINISTRATIVE TEAM

Rev. Brian K. Milford. . . . .President and Publisher

Marjorie M. Pon . Associate Publisher and Editor of Church School Publications

Cover design by *Celebrate Wonder* Design Team. Cover photos: Shutterstock; cover illustrations: Brave Union.

Art Credits: pp. 9, 10, 12, 13, 14, 17, 22, 23, 26, 27, 28: Shutterstock; p. 15: Becky Fawson/Gwen Walters; p. 25: Mark Collins/Illustration Online LLC; pp. 3, 19: Mary Grace Corpus/Gwen Walters; pp. 7, 8, 20, 24: Brave Union/Illustration Online LLC; p. 18: UNICEF, Cecil Bo Dzwowa/Shutterstock.com; pp. 5, 11: Matt Orozco Background art unless otherwise noted: Shutterstock

CELEBRATE WONDER ALL AGES, TAKE HOME ACTIVITY SHEETS: An official resource for The United Methodist Church approved by Discipleship Ministries and published quarterly by Abingdon Press, a division of The United Methodist Publishing House, 810 12th Avenue South, Nashville TN 37203. Copyright © 2023 Abingdon Press. All rights reserved. Printed in the United States of America.

To order copies of this publication, call toll free: **800-672-1789**. You may fax your order to 800-445-8189. Telecommunication Device for the Deaf/Telex Telephone: 800-227-4091. Or order online at **cokesbury.com**. Use your Cokesbury account, Visa, Discover, or Mastercard.

For information concerning permission to reproduce any material in this publication, write to Rights and Permissions, The United Methodist Publishing House, 810 12th Avenue South, Nashville TN 37203.

You may also fax your request to 615-749-6128 or email *permissions@umpublishing.org*.

COMMON ENGLISH BIBLE Scripture quotations are taken from the Common English Bible, copyright 2011. Used by permission. All rights reserved.

CONTENT

T0011716

SCOPE AND SEQUENCE FALL 2023–SUMMER 2024

Fall 2023	Winter 2023–24	Spring 2024	Summer 2024
UNIT 1: CREATIVITY	**UNIT 1: JOY**	**UNIT 1: REMEMBER**	**UNIT 1: PEACE**
God Creates the Earth Genesis 1:1-19	Mary's Joy Luke 1:26-38, 46-56	Jesus Washes Feet John 13:1-17	Abraham and Lot Genesis 13:1-18
God Creates Living Things Genesis 1:20-25	Joseph's Joy Matthew 1:18-24	The Last Supper Luke 22:14-20	David and Abigail 1 Samuel 25:1-42
God Creates People Genesis 1:26–2:4	Jesus Brings Joy Luke 2:1-7	Praying in the Garden Luke 22:39-46	Be Peaceful Psalm 23:1-6
God Creates Helpers Genesis 2:10-23	Joyous News Luke 2:8-20	Jesus Enters Jerusalem Matthew 21:1-11	Esther Book of Esther
	The Magi Matthew 2:1-12	Resurrection Matthew 28:1-10	Peacemakers Matthew 5:1-12
UNIT 2: FAITH	**UNIT 2: INCLUDE**	**UNIT 2: SHARE**	**UNIT 2: BELONG**
Abraham and Sarah Genesis 12:1-9	Jesus' Baptism Matthew 3:13-17	The Great Commission Matthew 28:16-20	Babel Genesis 11:1-9
God's Promise to Abraham Genesis 15:1-6	Calling the Disciples Matthew 4:18-22	Peter and John Acts 3:1-10	Mephibosheth 2 Samuel 9:1-13
Abraham's Visitors Genesis 18:1-14	Showing Love Matthew 5:43-48	Believers Share Acts 4:32-3	The Woman at the Well John 4:4-30, 39-42
Isaac Is Born Genesis 21:1-7	God's Kingdom Luke 13:18-21	Choosing the Seven Acts 6:1-7	Peter's Dream Acts 10:1-48
Jacob and Esau Genesis 25:19-28			
UNIT 3: BLESSING	**UNIT 3: GUIDE**	**UNIT 3: LOVE**	**UNIT 3: COURAGE**
The Birthright Genesis 25:29-34	The Lord's Prayer Matthew 6:5-15	Peter and Tabitha Acts 9:36-43	Rahab Joshua 2:1-24
The Blessing Genesis 27:1-45	Jesus Calms the Storm Mark 4:35-41	The Church Grows Acts 9:26-31	Ruth and Naomi Book of Ruth
Jacob's Ladder Genesis 28:10-22	Mary and Martha Luke 10:38-42	Pentecost Acts 2:1-12	Mary Anoints Jesus John 12:1-8
A Peaceable Kingdom Isaiah 11:6-9	Zacchaeus Luke 19:1-10	Love in Action Romans 12:9-18	Lydia Acts 16:11-15

Abraham and Lot
You Can Go Your Own Way

Abraham and Lot are going in two different directions. Help each of them follow his own path.

Abraham and Lot
Story Words

Search the puzzle for the words in the word bank, which are from our Bible story (Genesis 13:1-18).

```
E  L  T  T  A  C  E  F  I  F  S  Q  S  O  A
C  A  H  I  A  B  F  W  L  Z  T  S  N  Y  X
F  D  M  Z  G  Q  R  O  K  S  N  G  O  J  K
Y  Q  Y  N  G  Y  C  C  S  O  E  K  I  T  O
I  L  E  B  T  K  O  P  J  O  T  I  S  Z  I
U  J  W  B  S  T  R  S  W  V  G  X  S  A  R
Y  B  B  D  S  N  F  O  C  V  H  B  E  S  Q
I  I  I  E  R  R  P  J  W  P  E  R  S  T  X
E  R  V  D  X  W  A  Z  J  O  R  F  S  Y  E
A  I  Z  K  F  D  E  T  J  R  D  D  O  L  I
L  M  A  X  S  D  Z  A  L  V  I  B  P  C  E
C  W  C  L  W  D  Y  A  L  A  N  Z  M  B  N
E  B  Y  F  E  B  C  O  D  T  G  J  X  A  I
L  F  Y  D  I  T  Z  H  F  A  H  M  H  C  H
C  O  N  F  L  I  C  T  S  I  Z  Y  L  B  Y
```

Word Bank

ALTAR	CATTLE	FLOCKS	LIVESTOCK	TENTS
ARID	CONFLICTS	HERDING	POSSESSIONS	WEALTHY

Abraham and Lot

David and Abigail
Abigail's Peacemaking

Below are some steps for making peace. Look up 1 Samuel 25:1-42 in your Bible to find places in the story where Abigail completes each step. Write in each box the verse number where she completes the action.

1. Recognize that a wrong has been done.

2. Take steps to make the situation right.

3. Ask the person the wrong was done to if you may speak with him or her.

4. Apologize sincerely.

David and Abigail
When I Am Angry

Read each idea of how you can cool off when you are angry.
In the box below the sun, draw how you are feeling.

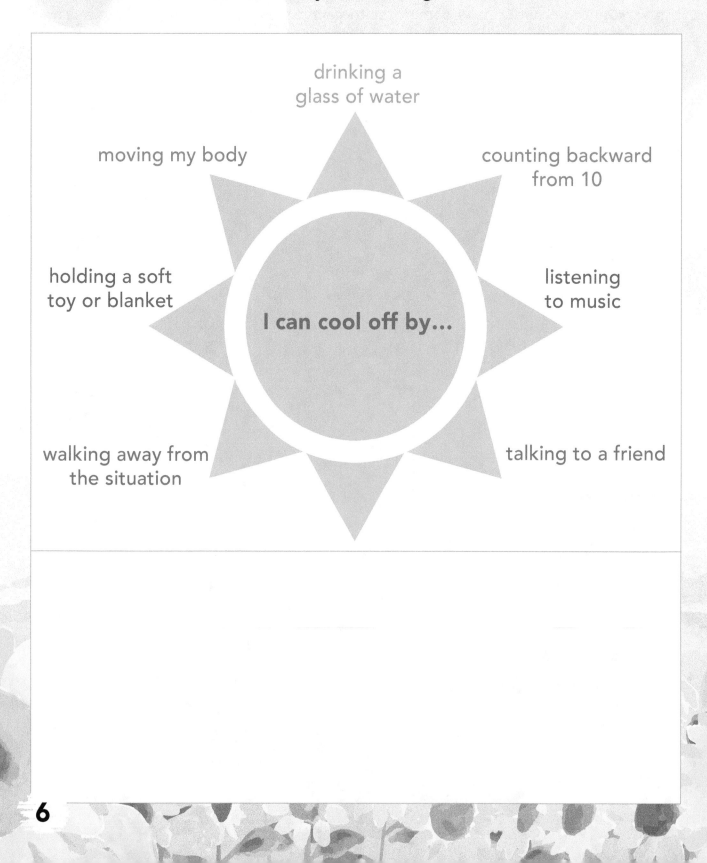

drinking a
glass of water

moving my body

counting backward
from 10

holding a soft
toy or blanket

I can cool off by...

listening
to music

walking away from
the situation

talking to a friend

Be Peaceful
My Peaceful Poem

Today's Bible story comes from the Book of Psalms. A psalm is like a poem that uses words to talk about God. Read today's psalm, Psalm 23. What do you want to say about God? Write it in your own poem or prayer.

Be Peaceful
The Lord Is My Shepherd

Read the article and respond to the question at the end.

Shepherding is a very old profession, but it still exists today. A shepherd is a person who is in charge of taking care of sheep. Shepherds keep the sheep safe from all harm, including protecting them from other animals. Shepherds raise sheep so that the sheep can provide resources for communities, such as wool and hides for making cloth and clothing and meat for food. Because sheep provided all these necessities, they were important to people in biblical times.

There are many references to shepherds in the Bible. Even King David was a shepherd before he became the king of Israel. Biblical people also referred to their leaders as shepherds.

Our Bible story uses a metaphor to explain how God is like a shepherd to us. A metaphor is a statement that uses a thing or idea in place of another thing or idea to suggest that the two things are alike. Our Scripture uses the metaphor "The Lord is my shepherd" (Psalm 23:1a).

What are some specific ways you think God is like a shepherd?

Esther
Jewish Feast

Find the extra letter in each line to discover a Jewish feast to commemorate the way Esther saved her people.

ABCDEFGHIJKLMNOPPQRSTUVWXYZ _____

ABCDEFGHIJKLMNOPQRSTUUVWXYZ _____

ABCDEFGHIJKLMNOPQRRSTUVWXYZ _____

ABCDEFGHIIJKLMNOPQRSTUVWXYZ _____

ABCDEFGHIJKLMMNOPQRSTUVWXYZ _____

Esther
Find the Bible Verse

Find the words in our Bible verse hidden in the picture. Write the verse in order in the box below.

Peacemakers
Beatitudes Wheel

Cut out the two parts of the wheel. Place the circle with the cutout on top of the other circle. Use a brad to connect the two circles together. Then turn the wheel to read the Beatitudes.

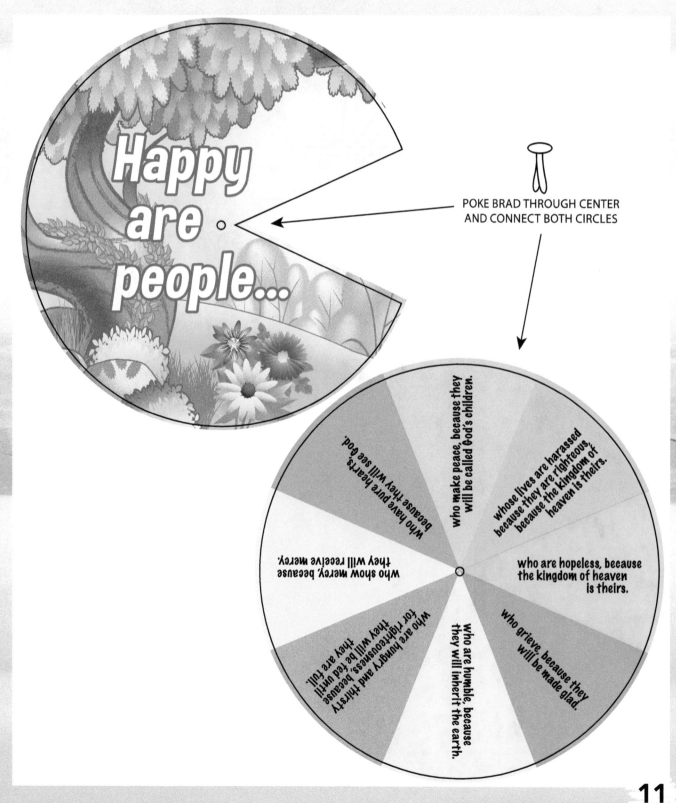

POKE BRAD THROUGH CENTER AND CONNECT BOTH CIRCLES

Happy are people...

who make peace, because they will be called God's children.

whose lives are harassed because they are righteous, because the kingdom of heaven is theirs.

who have pure hearts, because they will see God.

who are hopeless, because the kingdom of heaven is theirs.

who show mercy, because they will receive mercy.

who grieve because they will be made glad.

who are hungry and thirsty for righteousness, because they will be fed until they are full.

who are humble, because they will inherit the earth.

Babel
Tower-of-Babel Maze

Help each person find his way to a different part of the world.

Babel
Different Places

Draw a line from each country to the flag you think it goes with.

Brazil

Finland

India

France

Mexico

Egypt

14

Mephibosheth
Letters in His Name

Mephibosheth's name is long and has a lot of letters. Read the clues. Each answer starts with a letter in Mephibosheth's name, and one letter has been provided for you.

To get together with someone (verb)   ___ e ___ ___

Two people who are in agreement (pronoun)   ___ ___ ___ h

Something that's hard to climb out of (noun)   p ___ ___

What shepherds take care of (noun)   ___ h ___ ___ ___

To want something to happen (verb)   ___ ___ p ___

The pointed end of something (noun)   ___ i ___

Something used with water to clean floors (noun)   ___ ___ p

Another word for a warm climate (adjective)   ___ o ___

An animal a human keeps in the house (noun)   ___ ___ t

Something you wear on your foot (noun)   ___ ___ ___ e

Mephibosheth

At Your Table

Who would you want to share a meal with? Are there special people you would want to invite to eat with you? Write or draw about it.

The Woman at the Well
History Between Samaritans and Jews

Read the article and then respond to the reflection questions.

The group of people in the Bible known as Samaritans were from a place called Samaria. Many Samaritans did not follow the Law (rules for living together in a community), and they did not participate in Hebrew worship practices. This included not recognizing Jerusalem as the proper place to worship, as the Jews did. The Samaritans instead made Mount Gerizim their central worship place.

The Jews had been exiled and sent to Babylon after Babylon conquered Judah. When the Jews who had been exiled were allowed to return to Judah years later, they found that the leaders of Samaria were against rebuilding Jerusalem and the temple there. The temple had been destroyed when Babylon conquered the area. Because Jerusalem was a holy city to Judaism, the Samaritans did not honor it. The Jews felt betrayed, and the location of the proper place to worship became a cause of tension between the Samaritans and the Jews.

Can you think of any other situations in history when groups of people disagreed because of their different beliefs?

What do you think people should do to resolve conflicts over different beliefs?

The Woman at the Well
Finding Jesus

The woman in our Bible story met Jesus at a well. Solve the maze to help the woman get to Jesus.

Peter's Dream

Seeing My Dreams

Cut out the picture on the outer solid lines, and then accordion-fold it. Look at the picture from the left side. What do you see? Look at the picture from the right side. What is Peter dreaming about?

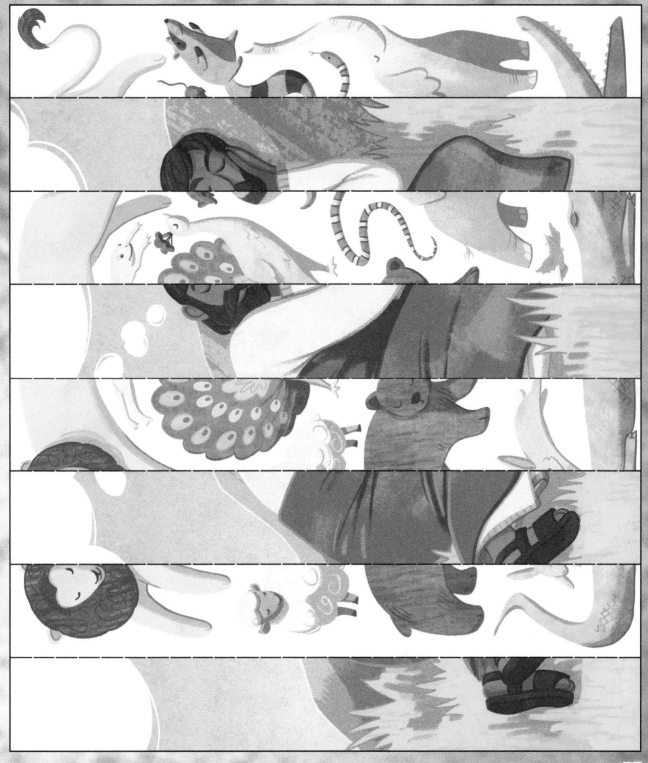

Rahab
Spy Escape Clues

Search for the key words in the word bank, which are from the spies' escape story (Joshua 2:1-24).

Word Bank

RAHAB	FORDS	HIGHLANDS
ROOF	ROPE	THREE
FLAX	WINDOW	
JORDAN	WALL	

```
J V V E J X Z K J S Y G U Y W
H C U E O F L A X K D N Q I S
H H G R R W Z O J W D R N Z T
W I Z H D K A V C I P D O G O
Y C G T A E V F C V O L Z F Y
Q F E H N G O E Q W J O V A F
F S B G L O U F H N P H V A V
N O X M R A Z D L W B A H A R
V V U D Q Y N H H J C T I J J
R N L V U Z X D B H F V W I W
J O X R Q Y T N S K E U J C N
S D P Q N X H F D M L L N W E
C M S E V Q R Z V Q X Z B A I
Y S V L F A L E W D M J R L S
V E U T S U I H A K G Q V L L
```

Rahab
Discipline

Our spiritual practice this week is exploring courage through discipline. One way to find courage is by studying brave people in the Bible. Each day, read the story in Joshua 2:1-24 and write your thoughts and feelings about the story. Each time you read the story, you might notice something new.

Monday
Reflections:

Tuesday
Reflections:

Wednesday
Reflections:

Thursday
Reflections:

Friday
Reflections:

Saturday
Reflections:

Sunday
Reflections:

Ruth and Naomi
Courageous Women Scramble

Use your Bible to look up the Scripture passages below to find out which courageous Bible woman's name is scrambled.

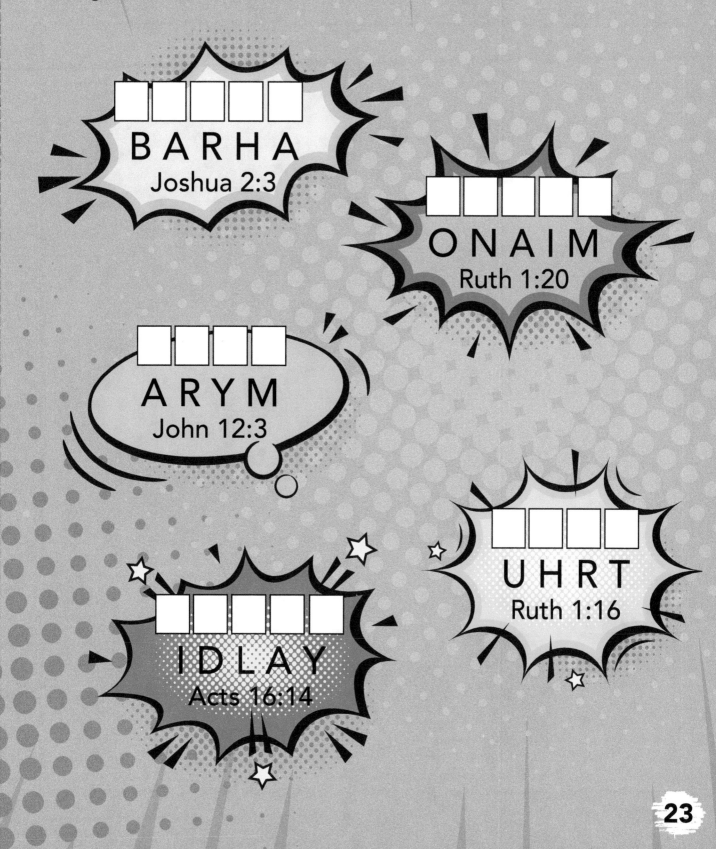

Ruth and Naomi
Courageous Women

Do you have special women in your life? What women help you, teach you, and guide you? Write or draw about these special women.

Mary Anoints Jesus
Ways to Serve Jesus

In our Bible story, Mary used her hands and hair to serve Jesus. Finish the sentences with ways you can use your body to serve Jesus.

I can use my hands to serve by…

I can use my feet to serve by…

I can use my brain to serve by…

I can use my voice to serve by…

I can use my ears to serve by…

I can use my eyes to serve by…

Mary Anoints Jesus
Search the Jar

Search the puzzle for the words in the word bank, which are from our Bible story (John 12:1-8).

```
H B R O L G S O J E S U S
M A H U J I V A N Q F
F N M A Z K R G X
S X F R I E N D S
J K V U P N F I S
I Q G A W Z L N R
M U L R X N O P J
J A F H J G M S E G U
L P R E N L A Z A R U S I
A H K Y B O Q A L N F B O K L
Q Z J T R K W O F Z U P V O R
Y D M S N M O U B N A M J F I L T
M O I B F W I J G O X E T A O O B
F A N N R J V N S M Z W H A R N J
E M T B N K O J T A G O G U H E M
E J N H M E X P E N S I V E M J S
T B R B P G R X B N J J N M A N B
O M Q Z A Q T O E K V Z O S R L P
F A N O I N T E D S S B W T R
M S W H U N R P L G X F H
V I X M V W B Q A I H Z A
B N L A P H X S O I G
```

FRIENDS	MARTHA	PERFUME
JESUS	DINNER	FEET
LAZARUS	JAR	ANOINTED
MARY	EXPENSIVE	HAIR

Lydia
About Lydia

Read the article about Lydia, and then reflect on what you learned by responding to the questions on the next page.

Lydia was from Thyatira in Asia Minor. Lydia was an independent woman and sold purple-dyed cloth in Philippi. Purple cloth was expensive and usually was worn by those in the upper classes of society. For this reason, it is believed that Lydia was a rich woman. She was the head of her own household, although it is not certain whether she was single or a widow.

Though Lydia was a Gentile, she worshipped with the Jews. When Lydia heard Paul preach, she decided to become a Christian. Lydia and her entire household were baptized.

Lydia was supportive of the church. She helped Paul and his companions when they were in Philippi by letting them stay in her home. Because she did this, they did not have to worry about earning money while they were there.

Today, there is a river in Philippi that flows with abundant cold water. The local people call it "the River of Lydia."

Write a list of traits you would use to describe Lydia.

Based on what you learned about Lydia in the article, compare and contrast Lydia with women today.

Answers

Abraham and Lot
You Can Go Your Own Way

Session 1 • Ages 7–12

Abraham and Lot are going in two different directions. Help each of them follow his own path.

3

Abraham and Lot
Story Words

Session 1 • Ages 7–12

Search the puzzle for the words in the word bank, which are from our Bible story (Genesis 13:1-18).

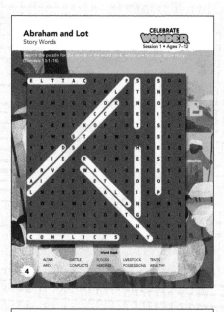

Word Bank

ALTAR	CATTLE	FLOCKS	LIVESTOCK	TENTS
ARID	CONFLICTS	HERDING	POSSESSIONS	WEALTHY

4

David and Abigail
Abigail's Peacemaking

Session 2 • Ages 7–12

Below are some steps for making peace. Look up 1 Samuel 25:1-42 in your Bible to find places in the story where Abigail completes each step. Write in each box the verse number where she completes the action.

14 — 1. Recognize that a wrong has been done.

18 — 2. Take steps to make the situation right.

24 — 3. Ask the person the wrong was done to if you may speak with him or her.

28 — 4. Apologize sincerely.

5

Esther
Jewish Feast

Session 4 • Ages 7–12

Find the extra letter in each line to discover a Jewish feast to commemorate the way Esther saved her people.

ABCDEFGHIJKLMNOPPQRSTUVWXYZ — **P**
ABCDEFGHIJKLMNOPQRSTUUVWXYZ — **U**
ABCDEFGHIJKLMNOPQRRSTUVWXYZ — **R**
ABCDEFGHIIJKLMNOPQRSTUVWXYZ — **I**
ABCDEFGHIJKLMMNOPQRSTUVWXYZ — **M**

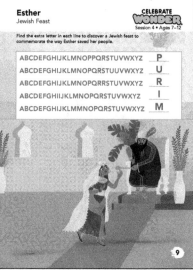

9

Esther
Find the Bible Verse

Session 4 • Ages 7–12

Find the words in our Bible verse hidden in the picture. Write the verse in order in the box below.

Happy are people who make peace, because they will be called God's children.

10

Babel
Tower-of-Babel Maze

Session 6 • Ages 7–12

Help each person find his way to a different part of the world.

13

29

Answers

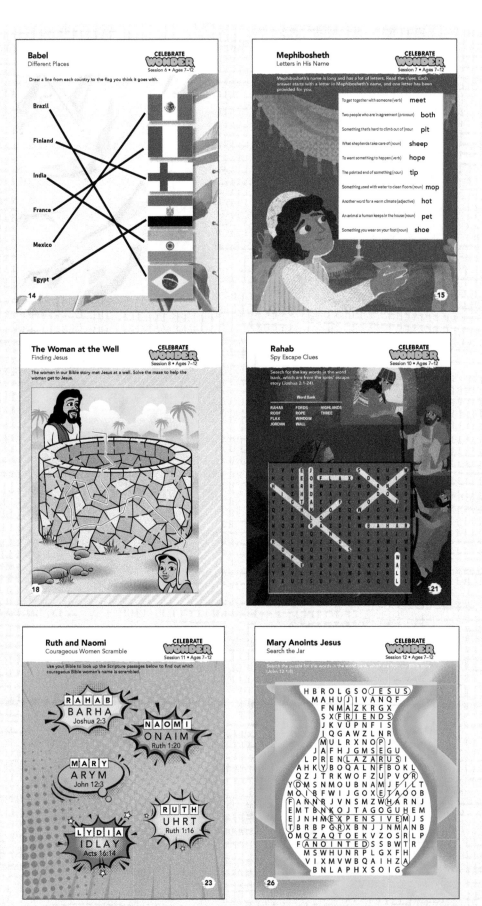

Printed in the USA
CPSIA information can be obtained
at www.ICGtesting.com
LVHW082352160224
772019LV00001B/2

9 781791 031220